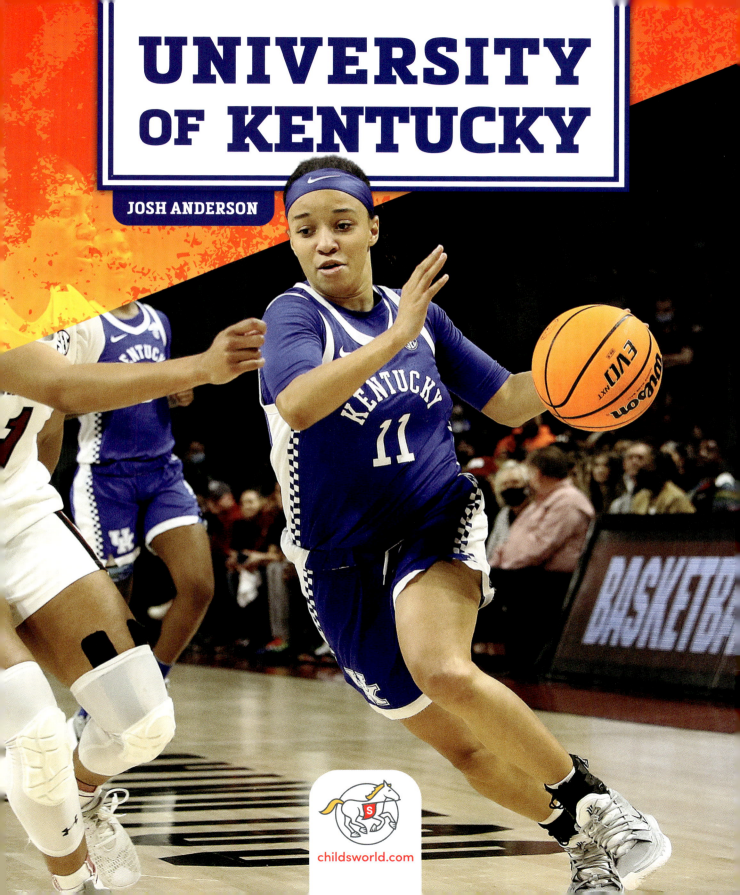

UNIVERSITY OF KENTUCKY

JOSH ANDERSON

Published by The Child's World®
800-599-READ • www.childsworld.com

Copyright © 2024 by The Child's World®
All rights reserved. No part of this book may be reproduced or utilized in any form or by any means without written permission from the publisher.

Photography Credits
page 1: ©Icon Sportswire/Contributor/Getty Images; page 2: ©Ethan Miller/Staff/Getty Images; page 5: ©Sporting News Archive/Contributor/Getty Images; page 7: ©Frederick Breedon/Contributor/Getty Images; page 8: ©Andy Lyons/Staff/Getty Images; page 9: ©Jacob Kupferman/Stringer/Getty Images; page 11: ©Eakin Howard/Stringer/Getty Images; page 12: ©Michael Hickey/Stringer/Getty Images; page 15: ©Matthew Stockman/Staff/Getty Images; page 16: ©Andy Lyons/Staff/Getty Images; page 17: ©Andy Lyons/Staff/Getty Images; page 18: ©Cooper Neill/Contributor/Getty Images; page 21: ©Bettmann/Contributor/Getty Images; page 23: ©Cheryl Chenet/Contributor/Getty Images; page 24: ©Rich Clarkson/Contributor/Getty Images; page 27: ©Eakin Howard/Stringer/Getty Images; page 28: ©Andy Lyons/Staff/Getty Images; page 29: ©Matthew Stockman/Staff/Getty Images

ISBN Information
9781503885165 (Reinforced Library Binding)
9781503885523 (Portable Document Format)
9781503886162 (Online Multi-user eBook)
9781503886803 (Electronic Publication)

LCCN 2023937880

Printed in the United States of America

ABOUT THE AUTHOR
Josh Anderson lives in the Los Angeles area with his two sons and a giant dog. He's been to tons of sporting events, but his favorite was seeing sumo wrestling in Tokyo, Japan.

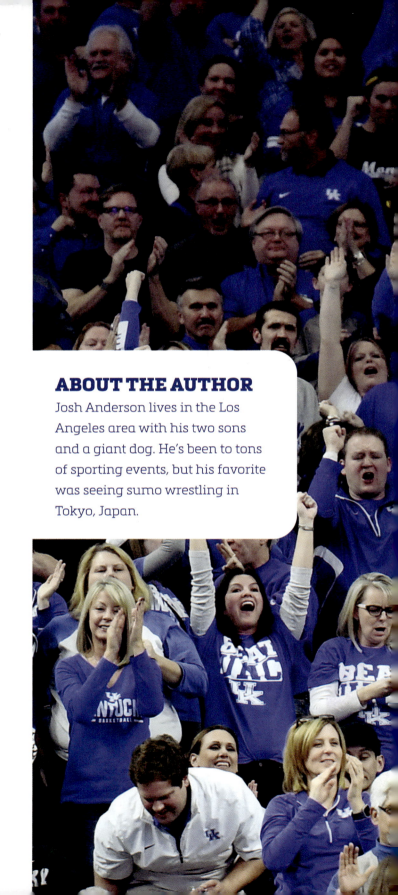

CONTENTS

CHAPTER ONE
Origins . . . 4

CHAPTER TWO
Rivalries . . . 10

CHAPTER THREE
Great Moments . . . 14

CHAPTER FOUR
All-Time Greats . . . 20

CHAPTER FIVE
The Modern Era . . . 26

Glossary . . . 30

Fun Facts . . . 31

One Stride Further . . . 31

Find Out More . . . 32

Index . . . 32

CHAPTER ONE

Origins

The Agricultural and Mechanical College of Kentucky opened in 1865 in Ashland. The school moved to Lexington, Kentucky, in 1878. Women began taking classes there in 1880. In 1916, the school became known as the University of Kentucky. Today, almost 33,000 students attend "UK" and root for the school's teams, which are called the Wildcats.

Men's basketball began at Kentucky in 1903. Legend has it that the school's first coach took up a collection from a group of students to buy a basketball. The cost was three dollars. The team played three games in 1903. The first game in school history was against Georgetown College. The Wildcats lost 15–6. Kentucky joined the Southern **Conference** in 1920 and played there until the end of the 1931–32 season. The next year, the Wildcats joined the **NCAA**'s newly formed Southeastern Conference (SEC). The Wildcats have been a force in the SEC ever since.

Kentucky center Bill Spivey takes a layup against Tennessee in 1951. ▶

Even though it was not an official school sport, Kentucky also had a women's basketball team in 1903. They played their first game that same year. Women's basketball became an official sport at Kentucky in 1974. That year, the Wildcats defeated Lexington 71–25 in the team's first official game. The women's Wildcats joined the SEC for the 1979–80 season. It was the first year the conference organized a league for women's basketball. The women's Wildcats were called the "Lady Kats" until the mid-1990s. They won the SEC title for the first time during the 1981–82 season. They also competed that year in the first women's **NCAA Tournament** and reached the **Elite Eight**.

University of Kentucky

TEAM NAME: Kentucky Wildcats

FIRST SEASON: 1903 (Men's Team); 1974–75 (Women's Team)

CONFERENCE: Southeastern Conference (SEC)

CONFERENCE CHAMPIONSHIPS: 56 (Men's Team); 3 (Women's Team)

HOME ARENA: Rupp Arena (Men's); Memorial Coliseum (Women's)

NCAA TOURNAMENT APPEARANCES: 60 (Men's Team); 17 (Women's Team)

NATIONAL CHAMPIONSHIPS: 8 (Men's Team); 0 (Women's Team)

Wildcat A'dia Mathies takes a shot over a University of Florida defender during the 2012 SEC Tournament.

ORIGIN OF TEAM NAME

The name "Wildcats" was first used for Kentucky's football team. The head of the military department at the school told a group of students that the team had "fought like wildcats." The name became popular and was eventually used for all of the school's sports programs. Kentucky's official colors of blue and white are even older than the team's nickname. They were adopted by the school in 1892.

The women's Wildcats have advanced to 11 of the last 13 NCAA Tournaments and are among the top competitors in the SEC most years. Although the team has never won a national championship or made it to the **Final Four**, the team has played in the Elite Eight four times.

The Kentucky men's team is one of the most successful in college basketball history. The team has won 75 percent of the games they have played. This is the highest of any school in the country. Their 61 appearances in the NCAA Tournament are more than any other team. Kentucky's eight national championships **rank** second only to UCLA, which has won 11 titles. And Kentucky's eight titles have come during five different decades—making them one of the most consistently powerful basketball schools of all time. The Wildcats have won the SEC title 54 times in the conference's 91 seasons of existence.

Kentucky freshman Cason Wallace (right) averaged 11.7 points and two steals per game during the 2022–23 season.

CHAPTER TWO

Rivalries

Rivals are teams who have a long history of playing each other for the right to claim they are the best. One of Kentucky's biggest rivals is the University of Florida. The two teams play twice every year during the SEC regular season schedule. Some years, they meet for a third time in the SEC conference tournament.

The first game between the men's teams took place in 1927 in Lexington, Kentucky. The Wildcats won 44–36. Kentucky and Florida have played each other 150 times, and Kentucky has won 109 of the matchups. But Florida is the only team to beat Kentucky seven meetings in a row. The losing streak for the Wildcats against Florida began in 2005 and ended in 2008.

The Wildcats women's basketball team played Florida for the first time in 1978. The Wildcats won the game 80–69. Overall, the teams have faced off 63 times. The Wildcats women's team has won 36 of the games.

Blair Green (right) and the Wildcats defeated rival Florida 72–57 in the 2023 SEC Tournament.

Kentucky's men's team has won their end-of-season conference tournament 33 times, often facing the Florida Gators during the competition.

The women's Wildcats played Florida in the first round of the 2023 SEC Conference Tournament. Forward Adebola Adeyeye scored 11 points and pulled down 17 rebounds. Both teams played with fierce energy, but Kentucky cruised to a 72–57 victory.

The men's Wildcats faced off with Florida in the 2011 SEC Tournament Final. Both teams were ranked in the top 15 in the country. And both had their sights set on going into the NCAA Tournament with a winning streak. Florida kept the game close, but Kentucky's squad proved too strong. Led by 17 points from guard Brandon Knight and 16 from forward Terrence Jones, Kentucky won 70–54.

Although they only play once per season in most years, Kentucky's other main rival is the University of Louisville Cardinals. The Wildcats women hold the edge over the Cardinals women with 34 wins to Louisville's 24. The Kentucky men's team has won 38 out of 55 games against the Cardinals. Six of those games were in the NCAA Tournament. Kentucky won four of them. The women's Wildcats have never played the Cardinals in the NCAA Tournament.

First Meeting:
1927 (Men's Teams); 1978 (Women's Teams)

Kentucky's Record against Florida:
109–41 (Men's); 36–27 (Women's)

CHAPTER THREE

Great Moments

Since the NCAA Tournament began in 1939, Kentucky has made it to the tournament more than 60 times. That is the most NCAA Tournament appearances in college basketball. The Wildcats have been a good team since the beginning, but there were times when they were the best in the country.

From the 1947–48 season through the 1950–51 season, coach Adolph Rupp's Wildcats earned a 125–12 record. They also won the NCAA Tournament three times.

Almost 50 years later, the men's Wildcats were once again a dominant team in the NCAA. The 1995–96 Kentucky team was one of the best in the sport's history. The Wildcats finished the season with a 34–2 record. They won the SEC with a 16–0 finish in the conference. Nine future National Basketball Association (NBA) players were on Kentucky's team that season. They included senior guard Tony Delk and sophomore forward Antoine Walker.

Antoine Walker (left) and Ron Mercer (right) helped lead the Wildcats to the NCAA title in 1996.

Guard Cameron Mills looks for a passing opportunity during the 1998 NCAA Elite Eight game against Duke.

The Wildcats won their first four games of the 1996 NCAA Tournament by an average of more than 28 points. They defeated top-ranked Massachusetts 81–74 in the Final Four. Then, in the final, the Wildcats beat Syracuse 76–67. It was Kentucky's first national championship since the 1977–78 season.

The following year, the Wildcats fell one win short of winning the NCAA title. They lost 84–79 to Arizona in the national championship game. After the 1996–97 season, Kentucky coach Rick Pitino became an NBA coach.

Under new coach Tubby Smith, the 1997–98 Wildcats became one of only five teams in history to play in three straight NCAA Tournament Finals. The Wildcats had a 35–4 record during the season and easily won their first three NCAA Tournament games. In the Elite Eight that year, the Wildcats' win over Duke went down in Kentucky history. With the Final Four on the line, the Wildcats trailed for nearly the whole game. Cameron Mills hit a three-pointer to give Kentucky its first lead of the day. The Wildcats held on for an 86–84 victory. Kentucky went on to win its second national title in three years, defeating Utah 78–69 in the final.

THAT'S STRANGE!

Former Kentucky player and broadcaster Mike Pratt passed away in 2022. The Wildcats retired his number 22 jersey at halftime during a 2023 game against Florida. After the game, Kentucky coach John Calipari pointed out some strange coincidences that happened involving Pratt's jersey number during that night's game. First, Florida's halftime score was 22, matching Pratt's number. Calipari also noted that the last player to score for Kentucky that night was Cason Wallace, who wears the number 22. Finally, the coach pointed to the final score of the game, which was a 72–67 Kentucky victory. Adding up all of those digits (7 + 2 + 6 + 7) equals . . . you guessed it . . . 22!

Kentucky's women's team battles with Baylor during a 2012 contest.

The Kentucky men's most recent national title was in 2012. Coach John Calipari led a team with seven future NBA players to a dominant 38–2 season. The Wildcats defeated rival Louisville and the Kansas Jayhawks on their way to the eighth national title in school history.

While the Kentucky women's team has never played in the Final Four, their greatest period of success was during the 2011–12 and 2012–13 seasons. Kentucky won the SEC title both seasons, tying in 2012–13 with Tennessee. Kentucky's overall record during the two seasons was 58–13.

The women's Wildcats defeated Gonzaga 79–62 in the 2012 NCAA Tournament **Sweet 16**. They advanced to the Elite Eight where they played the powerhouse Connecticut Huskies. Although the Wildcats lost, their season was one of the best in the school's history.

When Kentucky's women's team reached the Elite Eight round again in 2013, the Huskies were their opponent once again. Connecticut defeated the Wildcats 83–53 on their way to their first of four national titles in a row. The Wildcats women's team hasn't been back to the Elite Eight since 2013. But they have played in seven of the last nine NCAA Tournaments, making it to the Sweet 16 round twice.

CHAPTER FOUR

All-Time Greats

Starring for the Wildcats from 2010 to 2013, A'dia Mathies played in more games than any other player in the history of the Kentucky women's program. Mathies took the court 140 times for the Wildcats and scored 2,014 points. That ranks her third in school history. Her 320 steals are the most ever by a Wildcats women's player, and her 177 three-pointers rank fifth.

The Wildcats women's program lost one of its greatest players in 2022. Guard Rhyne Howard played four seasons for Kentucky. She ranks second all-time with 2,290 career points. Her 20.1 average points per game is also the second-highest in Kentucky history. Howard is also the school's all-time leader with 284 three-pointers scored.

Some of the brightest stars of the Kentucky men's program have been its head coaches. Adolph Rupp led the team for 41 seasons from 1931 to 1972. His 876 coaching victories rank eighth all-time.

Legendary coach Adolph Rupp draws up a play for his Wildcats. The arena where the men's team now plays is named for Rupp.

THE G.O.A.T.

There are very few key women's basketball records at Kentucky that Valerie Still does not own. Still was a center who played from 1979 to 1983. She scored 2,763 points and grabbed 1,525 rebounds during her career. Those totals are more than any other men's or women's Wildcat in school history. She was a three-time **All-American**. She finished the 1981–82 season ranked second among all players in the country in scoring and rebounding. Still helped lead the women's Wildcats to their highest ranking ever when they were fourth in the nation in 1983. After leaving Kentucky, Still played professionally in Europe and then in the Women's National Basketball Association (WNBA) for one season. In 2019, she became a member of the Women's Basketball Hall of Fame.

Rupp led Kentucky to their first four national titles. Four other coaches have led Kentucky to one championship each: Joe B. Hall, Rick Pitino, Tubby Smith, and current coach John Calipari. Calipari has been the Wildcats' head coach since 2010. He has led the team to the Final Four four times.

Guard Tony Delk played for the Wildcats men's team from 1992 to 1996. He was the leading scorer on Kentucky's 1996 National Championship team. Delk is the all-time leader in three-pointers with 283. He also ranks fifth all-time with 1,890 points scored. His 201 steals are the second most in school history.

Women's Basketball Hall of Famer Valerie Still starred for Kentucky in the late 1970s and early 1980s.

Even though Kenny Walker never won a national title as a Wildcat, he is one of the greatest players ever to play for Kentucky. Walker was a two-time SEC Conference Player of the Year, a two-time All-American, and a four-time All-SEC player. His 2,080 points rank second in school history. His 942 rebounds are the sixth most at UK. After his time at Kentucky, Walker was picked fifth overall in the 1986 NBA **Draft** by the New York Knicks.

Dan Issel is the greatest player in the history of the Kentucky men's program. Issel played three seasons for Adolph Rupp's Wildcats from 1967 to 1970. Even though he only played 83 games for the school, he is the all-time scoring leader for the men's basketball team with 2,138 career points. His average of 25.8 points per game is also the best ever for a Wildcats player. Issel is also the leading rebounder in school history. He grabbed 1,078 rebounds in his career for an average of 13 per game. Finally, Issel holds the school record for having 64 **double-double** games and scoring 30 or more points 31 times.

◀ **After his time at Kentucky, Dan Issel went on to become a seven-time NBA All-Star and Hall of Famer.**

CHAPTER FIVE

The Modern Era

Since she took over the Kentucky women's program in 2020, coach Kyra Elzy has led the Wildcats to the NCAA Tournament twice. In her first two seasons, Elzy had Rhyne Howard on the roster. Howard was the second-leading scorer in UK history. She graduated in 2022, and the Wildcats fell to last place in the SEC. But Elzy has hope for her team's future.

Kentucky's women's team has finished 12 of the last 14 seasons ranked among the top 25 teams in the country. The Wildcats have also played in 11 of the last 13 NCAA Tournaments. With guards Jada Walker and Maggie Scherr on the court, Elzy hopes to lead the Wildcats back to the top of the SEC and back to the national stage.

Coach Kyra Elzy led the Wildcats to victory in the 2022 SEC tournament.

After missing the NCAA Tournament in 2021, coach John Calipari's men's Wildcats have not made it past the second round in their last two tries. Calipari has been known for his recruiting during his time at Kentucky. That means he often convinces the best high school players to play basketball at Kentucky. Although many of these players leave for the NBA after only one or two seasons, Calipari continues to recruit a group each year that can play for the SEC title and make a run in the NCAA Tournament. Even though it has been more than 10 years since Kentucky's last national championship, the next one might be right around the corner.

Men's head coach John Calipari is known for bringing some of the top high school players in the country to Kentucky.

TEARING UP THE LEAGUE!

Like many of Kentucky's best men's basketball players, Shai Gilgeous-Alexander played only one season in Lexington. In 2017–18, "SGA" averaged 14.4 points and 5.1 **assists**, leading the Wildcats to the Sweet 16 round of the NCAA Tournament. In Gilgeous-Alexander's fifth NBA season with the Oklahoma City Thunder, he became one of the top scorers in **pro** basketball. During the 2022–23 season, SGA ranked fourth in the NBA with an average of 31.4 points per game. He was also chosen as an NBA **All-Star** for the first time that season.

GLOSSARY

All-American (ALL uh-MAYR-uh-kin) an athlete picked as one of the best amateurs in the United States

All-Star (ALL STAR) a player chosen as one of the best in a league, such as the NBA or WNBA

assists (uh-SISTZ) passes that lead directly to a basket

conference (KON-fuhr-enss) a group of teams that compete and play against each other every season

double-double (DUH-buhl DUH-buhl) a game in which a player accumulates more than 10 in 2 statistical categories (example: points and rebounds)

draft (DRAFT) a yearly event when the best amateur players are picked by professional teams

Elite Eight (uh-LEET AYT) games between the top eight teams in the NCAA Tournament

Final Four (FY-null FOR) games between the top four teams in the NCAA Tournament

NCAA (National Collegiate Athletic Association) a group that oversees college sports in the United States

NCAA Tournament (TUR-nuh-mint) a competition between 68 teams at the end of the college basketball season that decides the national champion

pro (PROH) short for *professional*, an athlete who is paid by their team

rank (RANK) to appear on a list of individuals or teams that have accomplished high statistics in a sport

Sweet 16 (SWEET six-TEEN) games between the top 16 teams in the NCAA Tournament

FUN FACTS

- Sarah Elliott blocked 195 shots for the Kentucky women's team from 2005 to 2008, the most in school history.

- Kentucky's men's team once beat Georgia 143–66. The 77-point victory is the most in school history.

- The longest winning streak in Kentucky women's basketball history is 17 games. The streak took place from November 2012 to January 2013.

- Jamaal Magloire blocked 268 shots from 1997 to 2000 for the men's team. That's the most in Kentucky history.

- The all-time assists leader in the history of the Kentucky women's program is Patty Jo Hedges. From 1980 to 1983, she dished out 731 of them.

ONE STRIDE FURTHER

- Kentucky men's coach John Calipari often brings the top high school players to Kentucky. But the players are often talented enough to leave for the NBA after only one season. How do you think it impacts the team to have so many players who are only in Lexington for one season? Write a paragraph explaining your answer.

- Write a list of your favorite college basketball players. Include two things about each player that make them your favorite. Is it the way they play? Their attitude on the court? What else?

- Ask your friends and family members about their favorite sport. Keep track, and make a graph to see which sport wins out.

FIND OUT MORE

IN THE LIBRARY

Berglund, Bruce. *Basketball GOATs: The Greatest Athletes of All Time.* New York, NY: Sports Illustrated Kids, 2022.

Buckley, Jr., James. *It's a Numbers Game! Basketball.* Washington, DC: National Geographic Kids, 2020.

Editors of *Sports Illustrated for Kids. My First Book of Basketball.* New York, NY: Sports Illustrated Kids, 2023.

Williamson, Ryan. *College Basketball Hot Streaks.* Parker, CO: The Child's World, 2020.

ON THE WEB

Visit our website for links about Kentucky basketball:

childsworld.com/links

Note to Parents, Caregivers, Teachers, and Librarians: We routinely verify our web links to make sure they are safe and active sites. So encourage your readers to check them out!

INDEX

Adeyeye, Adebola 12

Calipari, John 17, 19, 22, 29

Delk, Tony 14, 22

Elzy, Kyra 26–27

Gilgeous-Alexander, Shai 29

Hall, John B. 22

Howard, Rhyne 20, 26

Issel, Dan 25

Jones, Terrence 13

Knight, Brandon 13

Lexington, Kentucky 4, 6, 10, 29, 31

Mathies, A'dia 6, 20

Mills, Cameron 16–17

Pitino, Rick 17, 22

Rupp, Adolph 6, 14, 20–22, 25

Scherr, Maggie 26

Smith, Tubby 17, 22

Southeastern Conference 4, 6, 8, 10, 12–14, 19, 25–26, 29

Still, Valerie 22

University of Florida 6, 10, 12–13, 17